Elvis F

Quotes & Facts

By Blago Kirov

First Edition

*****

Elvis Presley: Quotes & Facts
*****

Table of Contents

Foreword

"I've come too far, and I don't know how to get back."

This book is an anthology of 90 quotes from Elvis Presley and 100 selected facts about Elvis Presley. It grants his reflections on subjects ranging from Ambition and Sin to God and Meaning of Life; in addition, the book shows the personality of Elvis into a different than legend, more human light.

Elvis Aaron Presley (1935-1977), often called "Elvis," was an American singer, musician, and actor who is considered one of the most influential figures in 20th-century rock and pop culture. Because of his success and charisma, he is also known as the "King of Rock' n' Roll" or only "King." Presley is probably the most successful solo artist in the world with over a billion records sold.

He began his career in 1954 as one of the first musicians of the Rockabilly movement, a fusion of "white" country music and "black" rhythm and blues. His debut came in 1956 when he became the controversially discussed idol of the rock 'n' roll movement. He caused a sensation with his extremely physical stage presence at a time when this was not yet part of the standard repertoire of live entertainers. Presley's trademarks were his distinctive voice, approximately three octaves in length, and his innovative, emotionally charged vocal style, with which he was successful in different genres such as rock, pop, country, gospel, and blues.

Presley was nominated fourteen times for the Grammy until 1978, which he won three times for his Gospel interpretations. At the age of 36, Elvis was the youngest artist to receive the Lifetime Achievement Award. Presley is the only artist, along with Michael Jackson, to be represented in five Halls of Fame: Rock' n' Roll, Rockabilly, Country, Blues, and Gospel. Six of Presley's song interpretations have also been recognized as historically significant in the Grammy Hall of Fame. According to the Recording Industry Association of America (RIAA), with 167 albums he has also received the most gold and platinum awards as well as a Diamond Award. The RIAA repeatedly honored him as "Best Selling Solo Artist in U.S. History."

In the American billboard charts, Presley took first place with 15 albums and 16 extended plays. He is the only musician in U.S. chart history with number one hits in Billboards Pop, Country, Rhythm & Blues as well as Adult Contemporary, and is the leader of Billboards "List of the 500 Most Successful Artists since 1955".

Between 1956 and 1969, Presley also appeared in 31 movies. Two documentaries about him appeared in 1970 and 1972; Elvis on Tour was awarded a Golden Globe Award for Best Documentary.

His Words

"I've come too far, and I don't know how to get back."

"Love me tender, love me sweet, never let me go."

"Ah just act the way ah feel."

"Ambition is a dream with a V8 engine."

"There's no such thing as an original sin."

"I never expected to be anybody important."

"Don't criticize what you don't understand, son. You never walked in that man's shoes."

"I'm not trying to be sexy. It's just my way of expressing myself when I move around."

"A live concert to me is exciting because of all the electricity that is generated in the crowd and on stage. It's my favorite part of the business, live concerts."

"After a hard day of basic training, you could eat a rattlesnake."

"Animals don't hate, and we're supposed to be smarter than them."

"Do something worth remembering."

"Do what's right for you, as long as it don't hurt no one."

"Every time I think that I'm getting old, and gradually going to the grave, something else happens."

"Fingerprints are like values--you leave them all over everything you do"

"From the time I was a kid, I always knew something was going to happen to me. Didn't know exactly what."

"I did the Ed Sullivan show four times. I did the Steve Allen show. I did the Jackie Gleason show."

"I don't do any vulgar movements."

"I don't know anything about music. In my line you don't have to. "

"I don't think I'm bad for people. If I did think I was bad for people, I would go back to driving a truck, and I really mean this."

"I happened to come along in the music business when there was no trend."

"I have no use for bodyguards, but I have a very special use for two highly trained certified public accountants."

"I hope I didn't bore you too much with my life story."

"I knew by heart all the dialogue of James Dean's films; I could watch Rebel Without a Cause a hundred times over."

"I learned how important it is to entertain people and give them a reason to come and watch you play."

"I like Brando's acting... and James Dean... and Richard Widmark. Quite a few of 'em I like."

"I like entertaining people. I really miss it."

"I like to sing ballads the way Eddie Fisher does and the way Perry Como does. But the way I'm singing now is what makes the money."

"I miss my singing career very much."

"I sure lost my musical direction in Hollywood. My songs were the same conveyer belt mass production, just like most of my movies were."

"I think I have something tonight that's not quite correct for evening wear. Blue suede shoes."

"I was an only child, and Mother was always right with me all my life. I used to get very angry at her when I was growing up-it's a natural thing."

"I was an overnight sensation."

"I was training to be an electrician. I suppose I got wired the wrong way round somewhere along the line."

"I'd just like to be treated like a regular customer."

"I'd rather go on hearing your lies, than to go on living without you."

"If you let your head get too big, it'll break your neck."

"I'll never feel comfortable taking a strong drink, and I'll never feel easy smoking a cigarette. I just don't think those things are right for me."

"I'll never make it, it will never happen, because they're never going to hear me 'cause they're screaming all the time."

"I'll stay in Memphis."

"I'm no hillbilly singer."

"I'm so nervous. I've always been nervous, ever since I was a kid."

"I'm strictly for Stevenson. I don't dig the intellectual bit, but I'm telling you, man, he knows the most."

"I'm trying to keep a level head. You have to be careful out in the world. It's so easy to get turned."

"It's human nature to gripe, but I'm going ahead and doing the best I can."

"I've been getting some bad publicity - but you got to expect that."

"I've never written a song in my life. It's all a big hoax."

"I've tried to lead a straight, clean life, not set any kind of a bad example."

"Just because I managed to do a little something, I don't want anyone back home to think I got the big head."

"Later on they send me to Hollywood. To make movies. It was all new to me. I was only 21 years old."

"Man, I really like Vegas."

"Man, I was tame compared to what they do now. Are you kidding? I didn't do anything but just jiggle."

"Man, that record came out and was real big in Memphis. They started playing it, and it got real big. Don't know why-the lyrics had no meaning."

"More than anything else, I want the folks back at home to think right of me."

"Music should be something that makes you gotta move, inside or outside."

"My movements, ma'am, are all leg movements. I don't do nothing with my body."

"Only thing worse than watching a bad movie is being in one."

"People ask me where I got my singing style. I didn't copy my style from anybody."

"People ask me where I got my singing style. I didn't copy my style from anybody.... Country music was always an influence on my kind of music."

"Rhythm is something you either have or don't have, but when you have it, you have it all over."

"Rock and roll music, if you like it, if you feel it, you can't help but move to it. That's what happens to me. I can't help it."

"Sad thing is, you can still love someone and be wrong for them."

"Since the beginning, it was just the same. The only difference, the crowds are bigger now."

"Singers come and go, but if you're a good actor, you can last a long time."

"Some people tap their feet, some people snap their fingers, and some people sway back and forth. I just sorta do 'em all together, I guess."

"That's why I hate to get started in these jam sessions. I'm always the last one to leave."

"The army teaches boys to think like men."

"The closest I ever came to getting married was just before I started singing. In fact, my first record saved my neck."

"The colored folks been singing it and playing it just like I'm doin' now, man, for more years than I know. I got it from them."

"The image is one thing and the human being is another. It's very hard to live up to an image, put it that way."

"The Lord can give, and the Lord can take away. I might be herding sheep next year."

"The next thing I knew, I was out of the service and making movies again. My first picture was called, GI Blues. I thought I was still in the army."

"There are too many people that depend on me. I'm too obligated. I'm in too far to get out."

"They put me on television. And the whole thing broke loose. It was wild, I tell ya for sure."

"Those movies sure got me into a rut."

"Those people in New York are not gonna change me none."

"To judge a man by his weakest link or deed is like judging the power of the ocean by one wave."

"Too much TV hurts movies."

"Truth is like the sun. You can shut it out for a time, but it ain't going away."

"Until we meet again, may God bless you as he has blessed me."

"Values are like fingerprints. Nobody's are the same, but you leave 'em all over everything you do"

"Whatever I will become will be what God has chosen for me."

"When I get married, it'll be no secret."

"When I got outta High School I was driving a truck. I was just a poor boy from Memphis, Memphis."

"When I was a boy, I always saw myself as a hero in comic books and in movies. I grew up believing this dream."

"When things go wrong, don't go with them."

"Where could I go but to the Lord?"

"Your kisses lift me higher...like the sweet song of a choir. You light my morning sky, with burning love."

Some Facts about Elvis Presley

Elvis Aaron Presley was a son of farmworker Vernon Elvis Presley (1916-1979) and textile worker Gladys Love Presley (née Smith; 1912-1958).

His twin brother Jesse (Jessie) Garon was born dead.

Presley's ancestors were mainly of Western European descent: on his father's side he descended from German or Scottish immigrants, on his mother's side from Scottish-Irish and French ancestors; a great-great-grandmother was Cherokee.

Elvis Presley grew up as a beloved and protected the only child. Parents and son formed an unusually close family relationship. Their social contacts took place primarily in the circle of the family and the immediate neighborhoods. There was no money for expensive leisure entertainment, and only a few people had a radio that was used in groups to listen to the country stars of the Grand Ole Opry.

The Presley's often provided for their entertainment by singing gospel songs with friends, which their son joined in as a toddler.

An uncle of Gladys Presley was a preacher in the Assembly of God Church, which the Presley's visited regularly and played a significant role in music.

Elvis Presley sang early in the Church choir.

The singing talent of the otherwise shy pupil caught the attention of a primary school teacher, whose initiative led to the ten-year-old boy taking part in a radio talent competition at the Mississippi-Alabama Fair and Dairy Show in Tupelo in 1945. After this performance, in which Elvis took fifth place with his a cappella singing, his parents gave him his first guitar.

Presley's passion for music found further nourishment in his admiration for country musician Carvel Lee Ausborn. He had achieved local fame as "Mississippi Slim" with his program at the local radio station WELO. Elvis was able to get his musical role model to let him sing in the talent show of his radio show and to give him guitar lessons.

In 1946/47 the Presley's family moved several times within Tupelos, as they could not pay the mortgage for their house and the rent for subsequent accommodations regularly.

Despite strict racial segregation laws, the Presley's family lived temporarily in a district of Tupelos, in whose immediate vicinity many African Americans lived. During this time, Presley made friends with a dark-skinned neighbor boy with whom he regularly attended African American church services - enthusiastic about gospel music - to sing along. Secret trips to the entertainment districts of the black population of Tupelo also awakened his fascination for the blues.

Hoping for a better economic future, the Presleys moved from Tupelo to Memphis, Tennessee in 1948. They lived there again in various pensions until they were allowed to move into an apartment in the Lauderdale Courts, a neighborhood of social housing in downtown Memphis specially built for low-income white people. Memphis had a lively local radio scene at the time, with "white" and "black" radio programs coexisting.

In his penultimate year at Humes High School in Memphis, Presley began to change his appearance by wearing eye-catching African American-style clothes and long hair with sideburns.

He also became increasingly enthusiastic about the gospel quartets of the Blackwood Brothers and the Statesmen. He was particularly taken with the Statesmen, who stood out for their emotional singing style, a thrilling stage show, and the charismatic lead singer Jake Hess.

Presley also went to the "All Night Gospel Singings" regularly during this time, where he listened to the lively Black Gospel.

The young Presley was not only enthusiastic about gospel quartets, blues, and country, but also about artists such as Ink Spots, Perry Como, Dean Martin, Mario Lanza, Roy Hamilton, and Metropolitan Opera Classics.

Shortly before Elvis Presley graduated from high school in June 1953, he took part in his school's talent competition, where he took first place with his vocal performance.

Immediately after receiving his high school diploma, Presley took a job at a small machine repair service in Memphis.

In June 1953, with his first salary in his pocket, he made his way to Sam Phillips Memphis Recording Service, a professional recording studio where each customer could record his record for a few dollars. Studio owner Sam Phillips had settled on Union Avenue in Memphis in 1950 and also operated his record label Sun Records, under which he successfully marketed mainly black R&B musicians such as Howlin' Wolf, B. B. King, Junior Parker, and Joe Hill Louis.

On Presley's first visit to Phillips' recording studio, he initially met only his assistant, whom he told he wanted to record a record as a gift for his mother. Marion Keisker was impressed by the vocal intensity of the recorded ballads My Happiness, and That's When Your Heartache Begins and noted down the name and address of the young artist.

At the end of 1953, Elvis took on a new job as a truck driver at Crown Electric, where he drove material to construction sites, helping the electricians working there as well. In his spare time, he earned a little extra with live performances at parties of schoolchildren and college students in the Memphis area.

In January 1954, Presley made his second visit to Sun. This time he met Sam Phillips and recorded - again at his own expense - the two country songs I'll Never Stand In Your Way and It Wouldn't Be The Same Without You. Phillips was also impressed and began to promote the young singer.

In early July 1954, Presley's first real recording session took place with guitarist Scotty Moore and bassist Bill Black, who at the time was trying to make a name for themselves with their band, the Starlite Wranglers. During this session, the trio first attempted to play several country songs without developing their style. Only when Presley took a break to sing the blues song, That's All Right Mama was a new sound born. That's All Right Mama is considered the first Rockabilly title in history, whereby Rockabilly as a fusion of "black" Rhythm & Blues and "white" Country is a variation of Rock' n' Roll.

The listener reactions to That's All Right Mama came immediately; a flood of calls and telegrams from enthusiastic listeners came in, leading to Dewey Phillips repeating the record several times in the same program.

After the success of That's All Right Mama, a B-side for a single had to be produced quickly. The choice fell on a reinterpretation of Bill Monroe's Blue Moon of Kentucky, which the trio transformed into a Rockabilly piece by changing tempo and speed.

By July 19, 1954, the day That's All Right, and Blue Moon of Kentucky was officially released on Sun Records as the A- and B-sides of single number 209, 6,000 orders had already been received.

In 1954/55, Sun Records made other well-known recordings for Presley, among them I Don't Care If the Sun Don't Shine, Baby Let's Play House, Good Rockin' Tonight, Mystery Train, I Forgot to Remember to Forget as well as Blue Moon, which was released on the album Elvis Presley in 1956.

Elvis Presley, Scotty Moore, and Bill Black had their first live performance together in front of a larger audience on July 30, 1954, at an open-air concert in Memphis' Overton Park amphitheater.

After this first resounding live success, Presley, Moore, and Black began to play regularly in clubs in and around Memphis, where they quickly became an underground sensation.

But Presley's performance at the Grand Ole Opry in Nashville at the beginning of October received a fierce reaction from the older audience, who were more interested in conservative country entertainers.

At the same time, The Hillbilly Cat and the Blue Moon Boys, consisting of Scotty Moore, Bill Black and the new drummer D. J. Fontana, toured the southern states with Presley. The musicians performed in shows with Hank Snow, Bill Haley, Johnny Cash, the Carter Family, Pat Boone, and Buddy Holly. Increasingly, Presley not only stole the show from other talents on these tours, but also established country artists such as Hank Snow, and created a fan base that soon included the young Roy Orbison. The intense touring activity of Presley and his Blue Moon Boys spread Rockabilly to the southern states of the USA and many musicians began to copy the style.

Sam Phillips gave in to RCA Records' advertising in November 1955 and sold his contract with 20-year-old Elvis Presley for the outrageous sum of $40,000, clearing the way for Presley's nationwide and international career.

Presley's switch from the regional Sun label to the national RCA label at the end of 1955 was the invention of Dutch-born Colonel Tom Parker. From the 1940s, he had become very successful as a promoter and manager of country stars such as Eddy Arnold and Hank Snow, with whom he also operated the artist agency Jamboree Attractions/Hank Snow Enterprises. After taking over Presley's management, Parker worked exclusively for Presley until 1977.

The first recording session, which took place on January 1956 at the RCA Studios in Nashville, brought the young artist several hits after initial doubts about his new label, including the song Heartbreak Hotel, which reached number one in both the pop and country charts in the spring of 1956 and became Presley's first golden record.

Presley's version of Hound Dog wrote music history because it was able to simultaneously position itself as number one in the American pop, rhythm and blues, and country music charts and became one of the first very successful crossover titles in US chart history.

In 1957, he achieved three more crossover chart tops with All Shook Up, Teddy Bear, and Jailhouse Rock.

Between January 1956 and 1957, Presley had a series of television appearances in various variety shows that were very popular in the USA at the time, which suddenly made him nationally and internationally famous. Among the shows, he appeared on were Jimmy and Tommy Dorsey's stage show, the Milton Berle Show, Steve Allen's newly founded show, and finally the number one vaudeville show, Ed Sullivan's show.

During a performance at Milton Berle on June 5, 1956, where he played Hound Dog, Presley made particularly rhythmic hip and leg movements during a slower blues part in front of the microphone. A national media riot of unprecedented proportions followed, and Presley has henceforth branded as "the personification of America's teenagers' corrupting rock 'n' roll movement." The performance was more or less interpreted as "striptease" on the open stage. Parents' associations, religious groups, and teacher organizations ran riot against the musician from the southern states. The heated controversy led to more TV shows ripping around "Elvis the Pelvis," which then censored him by filming him - as in one of Ed Sullivan's shows - only from the hip upwards.

Presley's international success gave him the title "King of Rock 'n' Roll" and the nickname "The Singing Quiff" because of his trademark hairstyle in some English-speaking South African countries like Kenya, Namibia, and South Africa.

One of Presley's first television appearances at the beginning of 1956 saw film producer Hal B. Wallis became aware of the young man from Memphis. Looking for a young talent who would attract the younger target group to the cinema, he was enthusiastic about Presley's charismatic appearance. Test shots and negotiations, which took place in the spring of 1956, quickly resulted in a contract for several films. Between 1956 and 1958 the feature films Love Me Tender, Loving You, Jailhouse Rock - Rhythmus hinter Gittern and Mein Leben ist der Rhythmus - King Creole were made.

Jailhouse Rock, in particular, is now regarded by film historians as a classic of its genre, which was entered into the American National Film Registry for culturally, historically and aesthetically significant films. The central vocal/dance scene with the title song by the well-known songwriter duo Jerry Leiber and Mike Stoller is also considered the archetype of rock/pop video.

In 1957 Presley led the American single charts for 21 weeks, an increase over 1956 with 18 weeks.

Parallel to film recordings, studio and soundtrack albums, Presley was on tour again and again during these years and was accompanied to his performances by police escorts because of the violent reactions of his fans. To keep the frenetic audience from storming the stage after Presley's gigs, the "Elvis has left the building" was born.

At the end of 1957, Presley received his official draft notice for military service, which he commented with the words: "It is a duty I got to fill, and I'm going to do it." Several military units made offers to use the young star for self-promotion. It was assumed that Presley, like many other celebrities before him, would at least choose the path to Special Services.

Presley completed his basic training in spring 1958 in Fort Hood, Texas - he was trained for use in a tank battalion.

On August 14, 1958, Presley's mother, who had been in poor health for some time, died of heart failure at the age of 46. Presley, who had a very close relationship with his parents, but especially with his mother, was devastated.

Presley served in the 1st Medium Tank Battalion/32nd Armor of the 3rd US Tank Division in Friedberg, Germany, from October 1, 1958, to March 2, 1960. In Germany, he first lived in the Hotel Grunewald in Bad Nauheim before renting a private house in Goethestraße 14 with his father and grandmother as well as two friends in the same place.

Soldiers who met Presley personally during his time in the army described him as a capable, very friendly, down-to-earth and generous despite his fame. Presley's military career is defined as successful - he showed leadership qualities, was promoted several times, his service record contained a series of commendations, and he left the army after two years with the rank of sergeant.

Presley discovered his love for karate, which he pursued with great dedication throughout his life.

According to various sources, he first came into contact with amphetamines in the army, which were handed out to soldiers in order, among other things, to hold out longer during maneuvers.

In September 1959 he met his later wife Priscilla Beaulieu at one of his parties in Goethestraße.

Between 1960 and early 1969 Presley made 27 films - mostly musical comedies - and a soundtrack album was released for almost every film.

Presley's appearance in Frank Sinatra's Timex TV Show at the end of March 1960 was his last television appearance until 1968.

After his benefit concert at the Bloch Arena in Honolulu at the end of March 1961, he only gave concerts again from 1969.

The close coupling of his career as a musician to a certain film genre led Presley into an artistic impasse in the mid-1960s. Although the demanding studio albums he released between 1960 and 1963 were well positioned in the charts and commercially successful, they were not as successful as the soundtracks of music films The soundtracks and the corresponding singles received much more attention from the films - their success led to more and more films, more and more soundtracks, and in 1964 to the temporary renunciation of new studio recordings.

1965 was the year the Beatles visited Presley at his home on Perugia Way in Los Angeles. No reporters and photographers were allowed to attend this secret meeting. Paul McCartney advised Elvis to release new songs instead of his mediocre films. In 1965, according to Elvis, he decided to give his career a new twist. This decision resulted in 1966 in the recording of the gospel album How Great Thou Art in Nashville, for which Elvis Presley received his first Grammy in 1967. The artistic highlight of the album is the title song arranged by Presley himself, in which he took over all four vocal parts of the gospel quartet classic and thus documented both his vocal ambitions and his love of gospel music. During this session, Presley also recorded Bob Dylan's Tomorrow Is a Long Time, an interpretation that Dylan said he valued highly.

The love song Are You Lonesome Tonight, was the only recording in Presley's career to be inspired by his manager Colonel Tom Parker and earned him three Grammy nominations.

On 1 May 1967 Presley married Priscilla Ann Beaulieu in Las Vegas, whom he had met in Germany at the end of 1959 and with whom he had lived since spring 1963.

Lisa Marie Presley, the only child they had together, was born in Memphis on February 1, 1968.

Presley gave over 1100 concerts from summer 1969 until his death on August 1977, of which over 800 took place at the International Hotel, today's Westgate Las Vegas Resort & Casino, in Las Vegas.

Presley's most famous concert, Aloha from Hawaii, was given in Honolulu in January 1973. It was the first concert of a solo entertainer to be broadcast live via satellite in numerous countries around the world and made him an international superstar.

In January 1969, Presley decided to record for the first time since 1955 in his home town of Memphis. The two albums From Elvis In Memphis and From Memphis to Vegas/From Vegas to Memphis were both in the top five of the country album charts and in the top 15 of the pop charts.

Presley's shows were always sold out and attracted a new audience to Las Vegas as fans from around the world traveled to see him live. Presley's last engagement in Las Vegas was on December 12, 1976, when he gave a total of 635 concerts in the gambling city between 1969 and 1977.

Less known than his connection to Las Vegas is that Presley was also regularly the attraction at the Sahara Tahoe Hotel on Lake Tahoe in Nevada between 1971 and 1976, where he also broke audience records.

Following his second Las Vegas engagement in February 1970, Elvis Presley gave six concerts at the Houston Astrodome in Texas, with which he broke new spectator records and which were the prelude to a touring marathon through the United States that did not stop until his death on August 1977.

The MGM concert documentary Elvis on Tour by Robert Abel and Pierre Adige from 1972 give a good insight into such a tour of the early seventies. The film, for which Presley gave the filmmakers one of his rare interviews, in which he at least gives a brief glimpse of the "man behind the image", recovered its cost within a matter of days, reached 13th place in Variety's Top 50 and received a Golden Globe Award for the best documentary.

At the time of the concerts in Madison Square Garden on June 1972, the frame of a typical Elvis Presley show of the seventies had already been set. It was not to change much in the following years, even though songs were exchanged again and again. The performance of certain songs at certain parts of the concert became increasingly ritual. The Elvis Presley show did not include any dance interludes or elaborate effects but was carried entirely by Presley's personality and performance - supported by the background musicians. No encores were granted, the opening act was usually a comedian followed by interpretations of the background singers, often the soul group Sweet Inspirations. Elvis Presley's typical stage costume at that time was the jumpsuit, a tailor-made, often white one-piece suit with a high collar, deep V-cut, wide legs, completed by a wide belt.

The Elvis Presley Show was never on tour outside the USA - a world tour appeared unprofitable in the early 1970s due to the 80-man stage troupe, the necessary safety precautions and the entertainer's reluctance to perform in open-air stadiums, which did not guarantee him the optimal sound.

In order to have Presley perform all over the world, the TV special Aloha From Hawaii was conceived, which was broadcast on 14 January 1973 in the International Convention Center Arena in Honolulu as the first concert of a solo entertainer by satellite almost around the globe. A total of over one billion people in over 40 countries are said to have watched Aloha from Hawaii. The concert appeared on the double album Aloha From Hawaii Via Satellite, reached number one in both the pop and the country charts in the USA and was also successful abroad.

He received his third Grammy for his interpretation of How Great Thou Art.

In 1970 Presley decided to record again in Studio B in Nashville. In five days he recorded 34 songs, which were released on four different albums between 1970 and 1972: That's The Way It Is (1970), Elvis Country (1971), Love Letters From Elvis (1971), and Elvis Now (1972). The A-sides on singles from this recording session, which is also known as the "Nashville Marathon," included You Don't Have to Say You Love Me, I Really Don't Want to Know, Life, and I've Lost You.

In 1971/72 Presley was back in the studio, recording songs for the gospel album He Touched Me in Nashville and Hollywood, for which he received another Grammy in 1973. In 1972 he also wrote Separate Ways and Burning Love in the RCA studio in Hollywood, both of which achieved high placings in the pop and adult contemporary charts.

In early 1972, his wife Priscilla separated from him, and the divorce was scheduled for October 1973.

Presley was taken to the Baptist Memorial Hospital in Memphis in mid-November 1973 in a life-threatening condition. The initial diagnosis was heart failure. It turned out, however, that Presley had undergone several weeks of treatment by a Californian physician due to his back problems, during which high doses of cortisone and Demerol were injected. This had not only led to a considerably bloated appearance and breathing difficulties but also addiction. In addition to the necessary detoxification, he was also treated for megacolon, hepatitis, a potential stomach ulcer, and chronic insomnia, from which he suffered as well as the so-called Morbus-Reiter Syndrome.

Treatment by several specialists led to a relatively rapid, albeit not complete, recovery and recovery phase. The admission session at Stax was continued from December 10, 1973, under better technical conditions. The recordings from the summer of 1973 appeared on the album Raised on Rock (1973), those from the winter session in 1973 on the albums Good Times (1974, number five on the country charts) and Promised Land (1975, number one on the country charts). If You Talk in Your Sleep, the ballad Its Midnight, Promised Land, I've Got a Thing About You Baby and My Boy, which was also very successful abroad, were successful in the single charts.

In 1975 Presley was back in the studio again - this time again in RCA's Studio C in Hollywood, where he recorded a whole series of tracks in March, including the dynamic T-R-O-U-B-L-E, all of which were released on the Today album.

Elvis Presley died on August 16, 1977, at the age of 42 on his estate Graceland in Memphis, Tennessee. His fiancée at the time, Ginger Alden, found him dead in the bathroom at 1:30 p.m.

He was buried in the Forrest Hill Cemetery next to his mother on August 18.

After attempting to steal the singer's body, the heirs received a special permit to bury Elvis and Gladys Presley at the beginning of October 1977 in the meditation garden of the Graceland estate.

In August, Presley's official cause of death was initially stated to be "cardiac arrhythmia due to undetermined heartbeat" (sudden cardiac death, arrhythmia). On October 21, 1977, after the completion of all investigations in the context of the autopsy privately commissioned by the family members, the office of the Shelby County Medical Examiner finally announced "hypertensive heart disease with coronary artery disease as a contributing factor" as the cause of death.

Some pathologists at the Baptist Memorial Hospital in Memphis who had obtained further toxicological reports did not agree with this announcement. They concluded that Presley had died not of heart disease but polypragmasia (i.e., taking too many drugs). The disagreement between pathologists at the Baptist Memorial Hospital and the coroner's team led to an expert dispute and legal controversy that lasted for nearly 20 years - fuelled by high media interest - including Presley's general practitioner in Memphis, George Nichopoulos.

Because of continuing rumors that the coroner's office had covered up facts or falsified the death certificate, the Tennessee State Health Department commissioned the independent pathologist Joseph Davies to conduct an official investigation into Presley's death in 1994. Davies, after reviewing all the records, came to the conclusion that medication had not played a role in Presley's death and primarily confirmed the cause of death of the 1977 Shelby County Medical Examiner.

Today, doctors believe that Presley's severe chronic bowel disease, which indicated Hirschsprung's disease and had long been the cause of treatment for the entertainer, was associated with sudden cardiac death.

Presley's voice has been counted among the greats of popular music and in the same breath with those of Al Jolson, Bing Crosby, Frank Sinatra, Ray Charles and B. B. King. Presley's vocal range is said by experts to be two and a half to three octaves. However, the range is not considered to be the main characteristic of his voice, which is instead characterized by an extraordinary range in voice coloration, which is why some called Presley a baritone, others a tenor.

According to music professor Gregory Sandows, Presley can be described as a "lyrical baritone," with exceptionally high and unexpectedly full low tones.

Music historian and critic Henry Pleasants also saw in Presley a baritone ("high baritone") - a voice which is best in its middle range and which achieves in ballads a "light, soft and seductive baritone quality" reminiscent of Bing Crosby, but "breathier and with a wide vibrato" similar to that of Billy Eckstine.

Another characteristic of Presley's voice is its versatility, which has enabled the singer to be successful in various musical genres that place entirely different demands on the voice. Thus, according to Henry Pleasants, from the beginning he was able to produce "the open, hoarse, ecstatic, screaming, lamenting, the daring sound of the black rhythm and blues singers" without being limited to this kind of singing. According to Pleasants, Elvis Presley had an "amazing voice - or more aptly said - many voices."

For Richard Middleton - professor of popular music - the remarkable thing about Presley's singing is not so much the obvious vocal versatility or the often quoted fusion of "white" and "black" musical styles, but the very individual vocal technique, which he characterizes as a combination of "romantic lyricism", "boogification" and "gospelization".

Closely connected with the vocal technique described by Richard Middleton is another, often quoted strength of Presley, to interpret even structured songs in a particularly exciting way. The message of the songs was always conveyed through the way they were sung and the emotionality they conveyed rather than through the lyrics. Singers and musicians who had worked with Presley said that he was particularly "soulful," which made him an extraordinarily effective mediator of emotions. Elvis Presley always placed emotional authenticity above impeccable vocal technique in the classical sense.

According to his statement, he never took singing lessons but sang from an early age at every opportunity with parents who had good voices of their own, with friends and relatives, listened to others, experimented a lot themselves, and otherwise relied entirely on his feelings and intuition.

His vocal skills are the reason why Presley is now revered by rock and pop greats such as Ian Gillan, Greg Lake, Bono, Robert Plant, Keith Richards, Bruce Springsteen, Bob Dylan, Elton John and the Beatles as well as classically trained singers such as tenor Plácido Domingo, New Zealand soprano Kiri Te Kanawa and bass-baritone Bryn Terfel.

The well-known music critic Will Friedwald sees Elvis Presley's originality and ingenuity above all in the way he combined the three musical directions Blues, Country, and traditional Pop to a very own style. This makes him one of the great stylists of the 20th century.

  Elvis Presley did not write or compose his songs himself, which is why some critics denied him artistic originality and authenticity in the past. Simon Frith, the sociologist, and popular music author, attributes this to the predominant perspective in classical musicology, in which text and composition traditionally take a higher place than voice and vocal technique and performance as such. Today, on the other hand, it is considered certain that Presley not only chose and arranged his song material, but also "wrote" it himself through his interpretation in a certain sense.

A song is only a song when it is sung, said Elvis Presley as early as 1956, thus emphasizing the fundamentally greater importance of vocal interpretation compared to composition. This is probably the main reason why Presley felt no urge to compose his songs in the classical sense: "No. I never wrote a song myself. I probably could have if I sat down and tried hard enough, but I never had that urge."

Like other well-known musicians before and after him (Irving Berlin), Elvis had an aversion to sheet music. So he emphasized that he always preferred "ear musicians" over "sheet musicians" because they were characterized by an intuitive and spontaneous approach to making music, to which he attached great importance. He described his selection process as "strictly intuitive" and "impulse-driven" without losing sight of the music market.

Elvis Presley quickly memorized the songs based on the demos, often changing the arrangements on the demos to better convey the essence of the song or to make the song "his" song. According to his music publishers and long-time composers, he always knew exactly what he wanted and proved an excellent sense for songs: "I'm telling you as a songwriter, he was the best singer for my money that ever sang popular songs. He could sing every kind of song. He made so many mediocre songs sound great. The minute you heard him sing, you knew it was him, man. And usually, that's only true of guys that write their material. When you wrote for Elvis Presley, you knew you were going to get a performance plus. He was one of those few people that when he recorded a song of yours, he would do it the way you envisioned it and then bring something else into it." - Doc Pomus, songwriter duo Pomus & Shuman

Between 1954 and 1977, Presley released 711 songs that appeared on about 60 original albums, 29 extended plays and an almost unmanageable number of greatest-hits, budget- and license-releases from outside companies.

Presley's song suppliers included professional songwriting duos such as Jerry Leiber & Mike Stoller and Doc Pomus & Mort Shuman, as well as "occasional writers" such as Mae Boren Axton and, from the 1960s, musicians like Mark James who cultivated their repertoire.

The musical background of the lyricists, who wrote in the Country, Blues, Rhythm and Blues, Gospel or Tin Pan Alley traditions, was also very different. Some wrote their songs directly for Presley, and others only learned after the release that he had made their song a hit. Some got to know Presley personally, a few could even accompany him recording their songs in the studio or watch his live performances of their song.

Presley never negotiated contracts himself during his career, and he concentrated entirely on the artistic aspect of his work.

The instrument with which Presley is primarily associated is the guitar. With an acoustic guitar, he was featured on numerous record covers, in most of his films and on stage. The image of the guitar-playing King of Rock 'n' Roll has inspired a whole next generation of rock musicians to learn this instrument, including Bruce Springsteen, Jimi Hendrix, Jimmy Page, Paul Simon, and others.

Presley himself didn't consider himself a particularly good or particularly bad guitarist, but throughout his career, he liked to make self-ironic remarks about his guitar skills: "I'd like to play this thing a little bit. Contrary to a lot of beliefs, I can play a little bit... a very little bit". "I'm going to play the guitar. I know three chords, believe it or not, I fake them all."

According to a number of musicians who had the opportunity to play with Presley themselves (including his lead guitarist James Burton and musician and composer Tony Joe White), Presley was an excellent rhythm guitarist who influenced the Rockabilly sound of the early Sun years not only on Scotty Moore but also on the guitar. However, Presley never appeared as a virtuoso and innovative lead guitarist; for him, the guitar was first and foremost an accompanying instrument and as such often acted only as a show element live.

Shortly after Presley received his first guitar at the age of eleven, he discovered another instrument for himself: the piano, which biographer Elaine Dundy calls his actual instrument. In contrast to playing the guitar, where numerous people taught him, he taught himself how to play the piano, even though the Presleys did not have their piano for a long time.

At the beginning of his musical career, Presley also played the piano in a whole series of early studio recordings and even during the well-known Million Dollar Quartet sessions in 1956. He can also be heard on the gospel album How Great Thou Art (1966), for which he received his first Grammy and other studio sessions from 1968 onwards. During rehearsals for the television comeback special from 1968, he relaxed by playing Beethoven's Moonlight Sonata, among other things.

Practically everywhere he stayed longer (also during his military time in Germany), he had a piano, because singing at the piano together with friends was one of his favorite leisure activities. From the 1970s he also sat at the piano in his concerts from time to time to accompany his singing especially in You'll Never Walk Alone and Unchained Melody. His piano playing on these occasions is called "staccato." Together with the respective vocal performance, it represented an emotional climax and was therefore very popular with concert visitors.

Besides guitar and piano, Presley also played electric bass. He can be heard, for example, on Fender Bass recording Treat Me Nice, b-side of the single Jailhouse Rock from 1957. Bass he also played with Paul McCartney during a visit of the Beatles to his house in Bel Air in 1965.

According to his statements, he also had a particular affinity for drums and the electronic organ.

During his time with the army, GI Presley also tried his hand at the accordion.

Elvis produced his records. He came to the sessions, picked the songs, and if something in the arrangement was changed, he was the one to change it.

His first experiences strongly influenced Presley's work in the recording studio in Sam Phillips' Sun Studio in the mid-1950s and the recording capabilities of that time. As a producer, Phillips' strategy was to provide his musicians with a framework for their creativity, without giving them any guidelines as to what and, above all, how they should play. He concentrated primarily on capturing the right moment for a recording without directly intervening in the creative process. It was customary at that time for singers and accompanying musicians to record the songs simultaneously in the recording studio.

For the early recording sessions, Presley met with his band, the Blue Moon Boys with Scotty Moore and Bill Black (later also D.J. Fontana), in the Sun-Studio. Only on location did the participants decide which songs they wanted to try out for a recording. Song lyrics (if not already known) were rehearsed on site, and the arrangements were worked out by the musicians themselves during the process. Nothing was read from the sheet, sheet music, and pre-made arrangements were undesirable. After all, the aim was not to play a technically perfectly arranged recording from the sheet, but to create a record that was as individual and spontaneous as possible, which, through "perfect imperfection," above all conveyed the feeling of a song in the best possible way. The studio sessions were accordingly unstructured. The musicians tried together until a point was reached at which all were resolved and free enough to realize this particular recording.

When Presley moved from independent label Sun to industry giant RCA at the end of 1955, he retained the way Sam Phillips taught him to work. Since A&R manager Steve Sholes, who was initially the official producer of the Presley sessions alongside Chet Atkins, initially had no access to his new artist's work, Presley took over the management of his studio recordings and from then on more or less produced himself without ever being mentioned as a producer on his records.

During the course of his career he was supported in his studio recordings by a number of personalities, such as the composer team Jerry Leiber/Mike Stoller, Steve Sholes and Chet Atkins, Chips Moman from American Sound Studio, Felton Jarvis, who in 1970 moved directly to Elvis Presley as an employee of RCA, and various sound engineers.

Presley preferring to record in the evening and at night. Even in later years, he did not like to sing his vocal part on tape in advance, as this set narrow limits to the spontaneity of all involved, even though this more modern method guaranteed better recordings in terms of sound technology.

Presley made all the significant decisions regarding the selection and production of his music himself, but once the single was in place, he was no longer involved in the marketing of his music. He left this to management and the record company.

Presley's frequently quoted live performance of Hound Dog on the Milton Berle show on June 5, 1956, is one of his most notable appearances of the time, triggering a national controversy that was sparked primarily by the singer's immoral movements. Movements which he defined in an interview in 1972 only as "body vibrations."

Relatively little is known that Presley conceived his version of Hound Dog in the spring of 1956 primarily as a humorous interlude for his concerts (a record recording was not planned at first) after he had seen a white vocal formation Freddie Bell & The Bellboys in Las Vegas. His performance confirmed the worst fears of the American middle class about rock 'n' roll and accused Presley of exhibitionist behavior.

Presley's live appearances on television were censored or defused, and at a concert in Florida in 1956, he was forbidden to move his lower body even in a suggestive way under the threat of imprisonment. As a substitute - strictly guarded by the local police - he only moved the little finger to the rhythm of his music.

When Elvis Presley unexpectedly died in 1977 at the age of 42, he left neither an autobiography nor any other records that could have been used to form a picture of him alongside his music.

Throughout his life, he wrote only a few letters, gave hardly any interviews and when he did, often in the course of press conferences, which rarely provided the right framework for a more in-depth conversation — questions about his private life or his political stance he always rejected in a friendly but firm manner.

Presley never appeared on talk shows, only socialized with a few select colleagues from the entertainment industry and avoided events such as award ceremonies or celebrity parties. Instead, he was repeatedly seen at concerts by colleagues in Las Vegas, in Memphis, in the press lounge at a football match or a karate tournament in the company of his ever-present following of employees and old friends - the press described them as the "Memphis Mafia."

Apart from the general data of a very successful career, little was known about the man from Memphis in the general public until 1977. This left much room for speculation, which encouraged the mythologization and ultimately also misinformation about Presley and which are now an integral part of his history as part of pop culture.

By the time of his death in August 1977, Elvis Presley is said to have sold between 400 and 500 million records worldwide; in the first year after his death, an estimated 200 million more were sold. According to some serious research, the figure was over one billion by 2007. Presley is thus considered probably the most commercially successful solo artist in the world.

The independent RIAA (Recording Industry Association of America) honored him in 2004 as Best Selling Solo Artist in U.S. History.

With 165 songs in the American Billboard pop charts between 1955 and 2008, Presley remains the undisputed leader in this chart category, followed by James Brown (107) and Ray Charles (91).

With a total of 80 weeks at number one, he still holds this record in the pop charts ahead of Madonna (79) and the Beatles (59).

Presley is the only musician who dominated the pop charts in two decades as the most successful solo artist with his songs. In the 1970s, he had to cede his top position to Elton John and ranked seventh. According to Billboard's classification system, Presley is the most successful musician in the pop charts between 1955 and 2008 - far ahead of the Beatles, Elton John, Madonna, and Mariah Carey.

Relatively little is known that Presley is also the third most successful performer of Christmas songs after Bing Crosby and Gene Autry.

Founded in 1957, NARAS honored Presley in 1971 as the youngest representative with the Lifetime Achievement Award, which honors the life's work of outstanding musicians of all genres and styles. After Bing Crosby, Frank Sinatra, Duke Ellington, Ella Fitzgerald, and Irving Berlin, Presley was the sixth winner of this award.

Presley was nominated fourteen times for the Grammy Award until 1978, which he received three times for gospel recordings. There were another five nominations for posthumously released box sets.

For his musical success, Presley received numerous other awards from home and abroad, which are exhibited alongside his gold and platinum records in Graceland.

Presley's former residence has been open for viewing since 1982 and was named a National Historic Landmark by the U.S. government for its historical significance.

Graceland has approximately 600,000 visitors annually.

Presley is the only artist to be represented in five Halls of Fame: Rock 'n' Roll, Rockabilly, Country, Blues, and Gospel.

In 1984 he posthumously received the W. C. Handy Award of the Blues Foundation in Memphis for his services to the blues as well as the Golden Hat Award of the Academy of Country Music.

Made in the USA
Las Vegas, NV
06 December 2022

61301462R00038